C000186207

"I cannot recommend this b
would read this book and do
so would transform our lives
our good and God's glory in

David Platt, Pastor, l
Founder, Radical; author, *Don't Hold Back*

"This may prove to be the most important book you read this year. For if you put it into practice, you will find yourself on a long-term course of Scripture memorization that will fructify your mind and heart for the rest of your life, and for all eternity."

D. A. Carson, Theologian-at-Large, The Gospel Coalition

"I recall listening spellbound to the testimony of a missionary who had recently been freed from prison in a country closed to gospel work and notoriously brutal in its treatment of Christians. Regularly beaten, often deprived of sleep, food, and water, this brother spent more than a year alone in a tiny cell. How did he survive emotionally and spiritually? He testified that it was Scripture that strengthened him and reminded him that he was never alone. Yet, he had no written copy of God's word. Instead, it was the words written on his mind and heart that carried him, the words he had committed to memory over his years as a disciple. In *How to Memorize Scripture for Life*, Andy Davis emphasizes the vital importance of Scripture memorization for obedience to the teachings of God's word and for growth as a disciple. He also provides practical instruction on how to carry out the Bible's explicit admonitions and encouragements toward memorization of its teachings. In our day, when retained knowledge has been replaced by an online search engine and the discipline of memorization largely forsaken, Davis's book is a gift to the church. Whether we are alone in a prison cell, standing to deliver a carefully prepared sermon, or doing the hard work of discipling a young believer, the Scriptures we have committed to memory will be the voice of God speaking to us and through us for his glory, our good, and the advance of the gospel."

Paul Chitwood, President, International Mission Board, Southern Baptist Convention

"I love Andy Davis and his Scripture-soaked ministry. In this book, he reveals his 'secret' behind a lost art in Christian circles—Scripture memorization. He is the right guy to write this book. He loves the Scripture, and he bleeds God's word in how he preaches, encourages, and talks. Reading this book will make you love the Scripture more too. Davis will show you how to get it in your mind and heart in ways that will transform your life."

J. D. Greear, Pastor, The Summit Church, Raleigh-Durham, North Carolina

"Andy Davis is my Scripture memory hero. He is a devoted husband and father of a large family. He pastors a large church. He writes books. And yet somehow in the midst of his busy life he has managed to memorize (at this writing) nearly the entire Bible. This little book contains his secret. It is life-changing."

Donald S. Whitney, Professor of Biblical Spirituality and Associate Dean, The Southern Baptist Theological Seminary; author, *Spiritual Disciplines for the Christian Life*; *Praying the Bible*; and *Family Worship*

"*How to Memorize Scripture for Life* is soul repair for the weary, battle armor for the war-torn, and a lifeline for backsliders. May the Lord use Andy Davis's life-changing book to raise up a generation of Christians who defy the trendy lies of the devil with the word hidden in their hearts. All Christians should read this book and practice its wise counsel."

Rosaria Butterfield, former Professor of English and Women's Studies, Syracuse University; author, *The Gospel Comes with a Housekey* and *Five Lies of Our Anti-Christian Age*

"Memorizing Scripture takes you deeper in your walk with the Lord and makes you better prepared to point others toward him. There are no shortcuts, but my friend Andy Davis has outlined some principles and suggestions that will help get you started and keep you on track in this profoundly rewarding journey."

Kevin Ezell, President, North American Mission Board, Southern Baptist Convention

"When many of us think of Andy Davis, we think of Scripture memory. Memorizing whole books of the Bible has been momentous for the whole of his Christian life and pastoral ministry, and he has long been a contagious and capable advocate for others doing the same. But perhaps even more impressive, when many of us think of Scripture memory, we think of Andy Davis. Few voices today, if any, rise so clearly to the top as both skilled teachers and practitioners of such an eternally significant topic."

David Mathis, Senior Teacher and Executive Editor, desiringGod. org; Pastor, Cities Church, Saint Paul, Minnesota; author, *Habits of Grace*

"Andy Davis is one of the most disciplined men I've ever met. So when I learned that he had much of the Bible memorized, I was not surprised. Still, I decided to quiz him. True to form, he went through the Scriptures from memory in a way that made me want to know Scripture like that! What you hold in your hand is what Davis has learned throughout a lifetime of Scripture memory. I can attest that it is helpful. So if you've wanted to memorize Scripture in larger portions and in a manner that you will remember, pick up this book and get to work."

Juan R. Sanchez, Senior Pastor, High Pointe Baptist Church, Austin, Texas; author, *Seven Dangers Facing Your Church*

How to Memorize Scripture for Life

How to Memorize
Scripture for Life

From One Verse to Entire Books

Andrew M. Davis

WHEATON, ILLINOIS

How to Memorize Scripture for Life: From One Verse to Entire Books

© 2024 by Andrew M. Davis

Published by Crossway
        1300 Crescent Street
        Wheaton, Illinois 60187

Cover design: Jordan Singer

First printing 2024

Printed in the United States of America

Trade paperback ISBN: 978-1-4335-9103-7
ePub ISBN: 978-1-4335-9105-1
PDF ISBN: 978-1-4335-9104-4

Library of Congress Cataloging-in-Publication Data

Names: Davis, Andrew M. (Andrew Martin), 1962- author.
Title: How to memorize scripture for life : from one verse to entire books / Andrew M. Davis.
Description: Wheaton, Illinois : Crossway, 2024.
Identifiers: LCCN 2023000658 (print) | LCCN 2023000659 (ebook) | ISBN 9781433591037 (trade paperback) | ISBN 9781433591044 (pdf) | ISBN 9781433591051 (epub)
Subjects: LCSH: Bible—Memorizing. | Christian life.
Classification: LCC BS617.7 .D38 2024 (print) | LCC BS617.7 (ebook) | DDC 220.07—dc23/eng/20230626
LC record available at https://lccn.loc.gov/2023000658
LC ebook record available at https://lccn.loc.gov/2023000659

Crossway is a publishing ministry of Good News Publishers.

VP		33	32	31	30	29	28	27	26	25	24
15	14	13	12	11	10	9	8	7	6	5	4	3	2	1

Contents

Preface

ONE HOT SUMMER DAY thirty-seven years ago, I was sit-
ting on a bench in Kenya waiting for a bus that wouldn't
come for hours. An idea popped into my mind that would
forever change the direction of my life: "Why don't you
redeem the time by memorizing the book of Ephesians?"
So I flipped open my pocket Bible and began a journey
of extended memorization that has continued to this
very day.

I cannot put into words the richness of that journey! The
insights that have flowed into my mind from the consistent
discipline of memorizing extended portions of Scripture have
been countless in number and limitless in significance. They
have revealed the staggering, even miraculous, depth of the
Bible—its deep interconnectedness, its refreshing truthful-
ness, its overwhelming beauty, its radiant hopefulness. More
than anything, the words that have been engraved in my mind
have delivered the person of Christ directly to my soul, and

by Christ I have known with increasing breadth and depth the glory of Almighty God.

One of the most stunning insights that came to me on that journey is that all truth encoded in words (nouns, verbs, adjectives, pronouns) is like seeing God "in a mirror dimly" and like so much baby talk (1 Cor. 13:11–12). For all eternity, heaven will expand and multiply our education in the glory of God, for then we will see him face-to-face. But for now, memorization of his flawless words will be the greatest and most eternally productive discipline you can embrace. My desire is that this little book will both inspire you to invest the labor and give you practical helps in how to do it.

May the ever-living and infinitely glorious God bless your meticulous labors in hiding his word in your heart. May he reveal himself to you in the person of his Son and in the power of his Spirit. And may he make you immeasurably wealthier in good works on that final day as a result, for the praise of his glory!

ANDREW M. DAVIS
Senior Pastor
First Baptist Church, Durham, NC

1

Scripture Memorization
Commanded

WELCOME TO THE RICH and challenging journey of Scripture memorization! You are about to embark on a searching and rewarding exercise of spiritual and mental labor: the memorizing of whole chapters and books of the Bible. This effort will challenge you greatly—not simply because memorizing is hard work (it is) but also because the verses themselves will search your soul with the light of God's perfect truth. Some days of memorizing are harder than others, and it becomes more difficult as you get older and busier. But the rewards of the knowledge of God's word, of growing intimacy with Christ, and of eternal fruitfulness for Christ will make all your labor in overcoming these challenges worthwhile.

As you face the challenges of extended memorization, it is good to be assured that God is leading you to do this. Scripture is clear that God does not want innovation when it comes to pleasing him; he wants simple obedience. "To obey is better than sacrifice" (1 Sam. 15:22). Jesus said, "If you love me, you will keep my commandments" (John 14:15). Yet the incredible beauty of the Christian life is that, in the new covenant, we know that the Lord will enable us to keep all his commandments by the power of the Holy Spirit. Ezekiel 36:27 promises that God will put his Spirit in us and move us to follow his commands and be careful to keep his laws. Therefore, in Christ all of God's commands become promises of what he is working in our lives now by the Spirit and what he will perfect in us in heaven.

But has God commanded us to memorize Scripture? I believe that a number of passages make clear that God wants us to commit his words to memory. And other scriptures openly encourage memorization as well. Let's look at some of those passages.

In John 15, Jesus likens himself to a vine and believers to branches that must abide (that is, live, dwell, or remain) in him in order to stay alive and be fruitful. In John 15:7–8, Jesus gets even more specific: "If you abide in me, and *my words abide in you*, ask whatever you wish, and it will be done for you. By this my Father is glorified, that you bear much fruit and so prove to be my disciples." For me, this is the strongest passage in the Bible on the role of Scripture memorization. Jesus describes the spiritual dynamic that produces the fruitfulness by which we will both glorify God and prove that we are Jesus's disciples. Abiding in Jesus by faith, moment by moment, is the key to everything. But what does it mean to have Jesus's "words" (plural) abiding (living, dwelling, or remaining) in us? It means at least that we know them, understand them, and can remember them. But more than that, it means that his words—all of them—are captivating our minds and hearts, spreading and permeating like yeast within us, dominating our lives more and more. This can be done as fully as Jesus intends through actual memorization of the word of God. By the way, I believe that when Jesus says "my words," he includes all of Scripture.

Similarly, we have Paul's commandment to the Colossians: "Let the word of Christ *dwell in you* richly, teaching and admonishing one another in all wisdom, singing psalms and hymns and spiritual songs, with thankfulness in your hearts to God" (Col. 3:16). By saturating our minds with the words of God and by continually keeping those words in front of us, we can best obey Paul's instructions.

Along with these passages come some from the Old Testament that speak of God's people "meditating" on God's word "day and night." Before the invention of the moveable-type

3

printing press by Johannes Gutenburg in the fifteenth century, Bibles were copied by hand and were extremely expensive. Only a small number of God's people would have had their own copies of God's word. So for most people, to "meditate day and night" on a passage meant to have memorized it first:

Blessed is the man
    who walks not in the counsel of the wicked,
nor stands in the way of sinners,
    nor sits in the seat of scoffers;
but his delight is in the law of the LORD,
    and *on his law he meditates day and night.*

He is like a tree
    planted by streams of water
that yields its fruit in its season,
    and its leaf does not wither.
In all that he does, he prospers. (Ps. 1:1–3)

This Book of the Law shall not depart from your mouth, but you shall *meditate on it day and night*, so that you may be careful to do according to all that is written in it. For then you will make your way prosperous, and then you will have good success. (Josh. 1:8)

Oh how I love your law!
It is my meditation all the day. (Ps. 119:97)

My eyes are awake before the watches of *the night,*
that I may meditate on your promise. (Ps. 119:148)

The same is true for us today, even in our blessed age in which the word of God is so readily accessible to many of God's people. Meditating on Scripture continually ("day and night" or "all day long") is greatly enhanced through memorization.

Along with this, some passages in Proverbs speak of treasuring or storing up God's commandments within us:

My son, if you receive my words
and *treasure up* my commandments with you,
making your ear attentive to wisdom
and inclining your heart to understanding;
yes, if you call out for insight
and raise your voice for understanding,
if you seek it like silver
and search for it as for hidden treasures,
then you will understand the fear of the LORD
and find the knowledge of God.
For the LORD gives wisdom;
from his mouth come knowledge and understanding;

he *stores up* sound wisdom for the upright;
    he is a shield to those who walk in integrity.
        (Prov. 2:1–7)

My son, keep my words
    and *treasure up* my commandments with you;
keep my commandments and live;
    keep my teaching as the apple of your eye;
bind them on your fingers;
    write them on the tablet of your heart. (Prov. 7:1–3)

If you read these two passages carefully, they seem to lead directly to the discipline of memorization. What does it mean to "treasure up" God's commandments "with you" apart from memorizing them? The second passage speaks of writing the teachings of God "on the tablet of your heart." That seems like memorization to me.

Perhaps one of the best-known verses on memorization comes from Psalm 119, that marvelous and complex poem of praise for the perfection of God's holy word. We have a clear recommendation of memorization, coupled with a powerful motive—personal holiness:

I have *stored up* your word in my heart,
    that I might not sin against you. (Ps. 119:11)

So also Deuteronomy 6 commands Jewish fathers to have God's word "on their hearts" and to "sharpen them" (the meaning of the Hebrew word translated "teach diligently") into their children:

And *these words* that I command you today *shall be on your heart*. You shall teach them diligently to your children, and shall talk of them when you sit in your house, and when you walk by the way, and when you lie down, and when you rise. (Deut. 6:6–7)

If you read these vital words carefully, the strong sense of memorization will come clearly to the fore. What does it mean to have these "words" (plural) *on our hearts*? I am not saying that memorization is either necessary or sufficient to fulfill this, but memorization of God's words is strongly implied and immensely helpful. And how can you talk about the commands of God continually with your children while walking along the road if you can't recite their content? The phrase "teach diligently" implies their continually repeated hearing of God's commands, all the time and in all circumstances. Like the honing of a blade by a whetstone, so is the repetition of God's words sharpening our children's minds and hearts. Again, that points to memorization.

Finally, consider the words of James 1:

But be doers of the word, and not hearers only, deceiving yourselves. For if anyone is a hearer of the word and not a doer, he is like a man who looks intently at his natural face in a mirror. For he looks at himself and goes away and at once forgets what he was like. But the one who *looks into the perfect law, the law of liberty, and perseveres, being no hearer who forgets but a doer who acts*, he will be blessed in his doing. (James 1:22–25)

What could be clearer than this? If we look intently into God's word and then *don't forget it*, what does that mean but memorization? And in this passage, such a habit is foundational to a lifestyle of obedience that is the goal of all Scripture's work in our lives.

2

The Benefits of Scripture Memorization

THERE ARE NUMEROUS SPIRITUAL BENEFITS to the memorization of Scripture. A proper assessment of these benefits begins with understanding the role of the written word of God in our lives and in our spiritual growth. First of all, our salvation begins in our souls by the gospel of Jesus Christ. By hearing and believing the words of the gospel, we are born again (John 3:3) and justified by faith in Christ (Gal. 2:16). Saving faith comes to individual sinners by hearing the word of Christ (Rom. 10:17). So the word of God is essential to our salvation from the very beginning. But Scripture also reveals that the way we make progress in our Christian faith is the same way we begin—by hearing God's word with faith (Col. 2:6–7).

Once we have come to life spiritually through faith in Christ, I believe that God has set before every Christian two infinite journeys: the internal journey of growth in holiness and the external journey of evangelism and missions. For this reason, my online ministry is called Two Journeys (www.two journeys.org).[1] Foundational to both of those journeys is the ongoing work of the word of God within us. By the word of God alone, we make progress toward Christlike holiness, and by the word alone, we win lost people to Christ.

The Internal Journey: Sanctification

Quoting from the Old Testament, Jesus Christ said that our spiritual life depends on the word of God as much as our physical life depends on food:

> Man shall not live by bread alone,
> but by every word that comes from the mouth of God
>   (Matt. 4:4).

Every word from the mouth of God is written in only one place: the Bible. Also, according to the apostle Peter, we have

---

1   See Andrew M. Davis, *An Infinite Journey: Growing toward Christlikeness* (Bingley, UK: Emerald, 2014). The journey in holiness and the journey in evangelism are infinite because they require God's infinite power, and they have an infinite (eternal) impact. Although we will complete both journeys, they will not be finished in this lifetime. We cannot retire from either of them while we live.

an ongoing responsibility to "grow in the grace and knowledge of our Lord and Savior Jesus Christ" (2 Pet. 3:18) and to "make every effort to supplement [our] faith with virtue, and virtue with knowledge" (2 Pet. 1:5).

But how are we to grow? Growth in the Lord is called "sanctification," the process by which we become more and more like Jesus Christ and more and more separated from the world. Christ says that happens by the word of God: "Sanctify them in the truth; your word is truth." (John 17:17). However, the word of God must enter us through our minds—through our understanding—in order to change our hearts. Thus, we are to meditate deeply on Scripture in order to understand it better, so that our hearts may be changed. And we are to meditate on "*every* word that comes from the mouth of God" (Matt. 4:4). There is no more useful discipline to this careful process of scriptural meditation than memorization. Memorization is not the same as meditation, but it is almost impossible for someone to memorize a passage of scripture without somewhat deepening his or her understanding of those verses. Plus, once the passage is memorized, a lifetime of reflection is available through ongoing review. Whether when you're driving on a long trip, walking alone on a beach, or even conversing with friends, memorized verses can flow within you and from you, causing a deepening of understanding.

Furthermore, these internalized verses also sanctify us by causing us to hate sin and to determine to fight it vigorously. Through memorization, we are able to stand in the moment of temptation through "the sword of the Spirit, which is the word of God" (Eph. 6:17). Therefore, the psalmist says,

How can a young man keep his way pure?
By guarding it according to your word. (Ps. 119:9)

I have stored up your word in my heart,
that I might not sin against you. (Ps. 119:11)

In addition, the word sanctifies us by transforming our entire worldview from worldly to heavenly: "Do not be conformed to this world, but be transformed by the renewal of your mind, that by testing you may discern what is the will of God, what is good and acceptable and perfect" (Rom. 12:2). The "renewal of your mind" happens by the flow of Scripture through it like a pure river. As this river of truth flows through your mind constantly, you will see things more and more the way God does if you are a child of God, for "we have the mind of Christ" (1 Cor. 2:16). This gives us more and more wisdom to deal with the evil of this present age.

However, this benefit does not merely bless *us* in our own growth and development but also becomes a treasure trove for the life and growth of others. One who memorizes Scripture will be used mightily by God to teach and encourage other Christians with an apt word from the perfect word of God: "Let the word of Christ dwell in you richly, teaching and admonishing one another in all wisdom" (Col. 3:16). How better can you obey this exhortation than through Scripture memorization? The "word of Christ" will indeed "dwell in you richly" as you memorize it and work it over in your mind through meditation. Then you will most certainly be useful to God in "teaching and admonishing" other brothers and sisters in Christ. Scripture builds the church to its final doctrinal and practical maturity (Eph. 4:13–16), and God uses those who memorize it to do this building in a powerful and eternally fruitful way.

For pastors whose regular ministry is the preaching of the word of God, no investment of time will be so richly repaid as memorizing whole books of the Bible. When the time comes to preach through a book of the Bible, think how deep and rich will be your preaching. Memorizing the whole book will give you a perspective on the entire message of the book (the forest, the big picture), as well as the details in each paragraph (the trees). My time in preparing new sermons from books I've already memorized is greatly reduced; or more accurately, I have already invested hundreds of hours into the sermon before I ever start to write it.

For me, one of the greatest delights in almost four decades of memorization has been the steady stream of new insights that come to my mind from memorization. Sometimes these insights come after I have reviewed the verses for months. Suddenly, light dawns in a new way on one of the verses, and I see things I've never seen before. This continually renews my love for Scripture and gives me a sense of the word of God being "living and active" (Heb. 4:12). These insights become the food I then pass on to people as I preach the word week after week from the pulpit. These same moments of thrilling illumination by the Holy Spirit are waiting for you as well. They are the nuggets of gold your mind will excavate from the mine of truth (the Bible) after hours of hard labor. These insights make it all worthwhile. Along with this thrilling journey of discovery is the ever-deepening sense I get of the stunning interconnectedness of the Bible as a whole. Only the perfect mind of God could have assembled these sixty-six books into one coherent message for the human race. I cannot adequately put into words how much the detailed work of Scripture memorization has given me this rock solid conviction that all Scripture is God-breathed and perfect.

Besides ministry of the word in formal settings, Christians of all sorts can be prepared to engage in excellent biblical counseling for their brothers and sisters. God will bring people to you to hear the wisdom he's stored up within you.

People who are battling secret sins, slipping into depression, struggling in their marriages, despairing about how to raise their teens in the Lord, or experiencing many other challenging circumstances will come to be fed and nourished by the word stored up in you.

The External Journey: Evangelism

The memorization of Scripture also enables us to bless lost people with an accurate and vivid presentation of the gospel of salvation. The gospel is "the power of God for salvation to everyone who believes" (Rom. 1:16). Those who memorize Scripture obey Peter's command in this regard: "Always [be] prepared to make a defense to anyone who asks you for a reason for the hope that is in you" (1 Pet. 3:15). The preparation Peter had in mind is powerfully done by memorizing Scripture. Remember that Scripture is able to make sinners "wise for salvation through faith in Christ Jesus" (2 Tim. 3:15). The apostle John said that the account he gave of Jesus's life in the Gospel of John was written so that his readers "may believe that Jesus is the Christ, the Son of God, and that by believing [they] may have life in his name" (John 20:31). So the words of the Bible are essential to winning lost sinners to eternal life in Christ.

The evangelizing Christian who stores up Scripture on the life of Christ can vividly retell some of the miracle stories in the

Gospels to a generation that is biblically illiterate and knows very little about the life of Christ. For example, having the account of the healing of the paralyzed man in Mark 2:1–12 memorized enables a Christian to captivate a hearer with the details of the miracle and cause that person to consider that Jesus has "authority on earth to forgive sins" (Mark 2:10). A believer can also explain the theology of salvation from Paul's epistles, if he or she has memorized those books. In short, Scripture memorization makes one a much more powerful and effective evangelist.

There are other benefits: power and intimacy in daily prayer, comfort during trials and bereavement, the development of heavenly mindedness, the manifestation of the fruit of the Spirit, conviction over indwelling sin, fruitful use of time while experiencing a delay, and more. Suffice it to say that this is well worth our time. When judgment day comes, we will regret the waste of a single moment not used for the glory of Christ. We will, however, not regret one moment we spent diligently studying God's word and hiding it in our hearts. We will only wish we'd invested more time.

3

Overcoming Excuses
for Not Memorizing

THE HUMAN HEART IS deceitful and twisted in so many
ways (Jer. 17:9). We can make amazing excuses for not doing
things that the Lord has commanded that would richly benefit
us. I want to briefly expose and refute a number of the more
common excuses for not memorizing Scripture:

"I Don't Have a Good Memory"

Actually, you have a much better memory than you think.
Consider how many song lyrics you have memorized—
many of which you don't even like! Consider how many
facts of history or literature are burned in your mind.
Consider how many phone numbers, addresses, and significant dates are written permanently on your heart. You

have a sufficiently good memory to begin memorizing Scripture. And the more you do, the better your memory will become.

"It Will Take Too Much Time"

This is really an exposure of your priority structures. We make time for whatever is truly important to us. I don't deny that memorizing books of the Bible is very time consuming, but it is also invaluable and rewarding.

"I'm Too Busy"

This is another version of the previous excuse. It all comes down to your priorities, to the value you place on the word of God and on your spiritual health. Admittedly, some seasons of life are busier than others, and in those times, your memorization may be greatly reduced. But a settled pattern of your life should be to work daily on memorizing Scripture.

"I'm Not Very Interested"

Ouch! This is one of the worst excuses of all. At least this individual is honest. But honest about what? That he or she has little interest in the word of God? Such an attitude reflects a heart that is in great spiritual danger and may even be unregenerate. A Christian loves the word of God and hungers for it.

"I've Tried Before, and It Never Really Worked"

Scripture memorization doesn't "work." *We* work. Memorization requires hard work, but God can give us the strength to do it by his Spirit. Scripture memorization is a discipline that will become stronger and stronger as we exercise our memory more and more.

"I Don't See the Benefit of Working on It That Hard"

The word of God is lavish in its promises of blessing to all who will trust it and follow it. Psalm 1:1–3 (quoted in chap. 1) promises that, if we meditate on God's word day and night, we will be blessed in whatever we do. What could be better than that? The New Testament links that blessing directly to the person and work of Jesus Christ. Through Scripture, we come to faith in Christ, and through Scripture we flourish in that faith. Nothing can make you spiritually richer than the word of God.

"If I Read the Bible Every Day, Why Do I Need to Memorize It?"

Obviously, it is true that a consistent pattern of reading the word of God is sufficient to feed your soul. A *broad* knowledge of the whole of God's word is vital. But memorization provides a *deep* knowledge. If we work very hard at memorization, we will memorize only a fraction of the overall Bible. We will get value out of whatever we read from God's word, but I believe the value is proportional to our understanding and internalization of the word. And the more deeply we meditate on and absorb those truths, the more profoundly we will be blessed.

"I Don't Know What Translation to Use"

The choice of a proper translation is a weighty one since we will be committed to that choice for years. There are no perfect translations, but in English, there are many excellent ones. I recommend that you research the strengths and weaknesses of the major translations and make a wise choice. Then go ahead and start memorizing—and don't look back.

"I Might Become Prideful"

The shocking news proclaimed by the Bible is that you're already prideful! We all are. Pride is deeply woven into the fabric of our sinful nature. The word of God is the remedy for pride, not its cause. If you struggle with pride, then memorize some verses on pride and/or humility. But to refrain from memorizing because you might become prideful is foolish. Rather, ask God to keep you humble as you learn the richness of his word.

"I Don't Know How to Do It"

That is what this book is for. I pray it will help you.

4

Memorizing Individual Verses
and Memorizing Books

I WANT TO BEGIN BY ENCOURAGING people who have never memorized any Scripture at all to begin somewhere. I started memorizing Scripture shortly after I came to faith in Christ my junior year at the Massachusetts Institute of Technology. My mentor encouraged me to use the Topical Memory System produced by The Navigators (www .navigators.org). It's an excellent approach to start memorizing the Bible. Other such systems are available as well, like Fighter Verses (www.fighterverses.com). So if you have never memorized any Scripture at all and feel daunted about taking on a whole book, I understand.

Memorizing key verses, like John 3:16 and 2 Corinthians 5:17, are great places to begin. The only problem is that memorizing individual verses has some limitations. Generally, people memorizing individual verses put them on little cards. Those who have been at it for a while have fifty cards or more. It begins to get pretty unwieldy. Plus, how do you choose what verses to memorize? And how do you remember what they are if they are taken from twenty different books of the Bible. At some point, I recommend transitioning to extended memorization of Scripture—that is, whole chapters and books of the Bible. Now let me make a defense for that approach.

Jesus said, "Man shall not live by bread alone, but by *every* word that comes from the mouth of God" (Matt. 4:4). Paul said, "*All* Scripture is breathed out by God and profitable for teaching, for reproof, for correction, and for training in righteousness" (2 Tim. 3:16). Paul told the Ephesian elders in Acts 20:27, "I did not shrink from declaring to you the *whole* counsel of God." Memorizing individual verses tends to miss less well-known verses that we might not feel are as significant. If we continue to focus only on our favorite passages of Scripture, we may overlook something new that God wants to say to us through a neglected portion of his word. God does not speak any word in vain, and no passages of Scripture are superfluous.

This approach also aids in the proper teaching of the word. The best mode of teaching and preaching is expository—setting forth in good order what God actually says, allowing the text to control the message. Preaching topically, while beneficial from time to time, is not the best long-term strategy of pulpit ministry, for the pastor or teacher will tend to say no more than what he already has understood from those favorite verses. But a pastor or teacher who works carefully through the passage as an expositor will open up a new world to his hearers, exciting them with observations they are not likely to have seen before. And since memorizing books leads to a constant discovery of new details and flashing insights, the pastor or teacher is able to keep the church's love for the word vibrant and thrilling.

Also, since much of Scripture is written to make a rational argument, the flow of thought is missed if only individual verses are memorized. But memorizing entire books verse by verse enables one to go easily from the trees (details) to the forest (big picture) and back again. This person will be able to tell you the overall flow of the book of Galatians, for example, as well as how each paragraph fits into this flow, and how each verse contributes to each paragraph. Thus, there is far less likelihood of taking verses out of context when entire books are memorized.

5

Getting Started

Making the Commitment before God

Go to the Lord in prayer and ask him specifically how he
wants you to invest time in Scripture memorization. Listen
to him, confident that he will guide you. Once you have that
sense from God, ask him humbly for help from the Holy
Spirit. Ask him to protect you from spiritual pride, for God
hates pride in every form (see Isa. 2:6–22; Luke 18:9–14).
Although knowledge of the Bible is absolutely essential to
spiritual maturity, such knowledge without love for God and
neighbor "puffs up" a person (1 Cor. 8:1), is useless to God,
and harms the church. Humbly make the commitment before
God that you will invest time in Scripture memorization.
Later, after you choose your book to memorize, you can make
a written covenant before God concerning your commitment
if that would be helpful for you.

Choosing Your First Book

The next step is to choose the book. This, too, should be done with prayer and a sense of the leadership of the Holy Spirit. Some practical concerns should guide your choice as well:

Not Too Long

Your first book should not be too long, lest you get discouraged along the way and give up. The greatest obstacle to a fruitful harvest in this arena is simply *giving up*. We abandon a course of action usually because the way seems too long and we feel that we lack the strength for the rest of the journey. Just as one who someday wants to finish a marathon does not begin training by simply running 26.2 miles but rather must work up to that level, so also with extended Scripture memorization. You must get the discipline deeply rooted in your daily habits, and you must develop your memory skills before you can attempt a really long book. Start with a book from 90 to 160 verses long. That is the range of most of the New Testament epistles. My opinion is that these epistles provide the best starting place since they give a lavish return for a relatively small investment. For people I mentor, I always start them in Paul's letter to the Ephesians—155 verses with lots of deep theology and practical Christian living.

Stirs Your Passions

Choose a book that God has used in the past to minister to you, and that you think would be most useful in your personal walk with Christ and in your ministry to others. You should also choose a book that still holds some mysteries for you to discover (as all Scripture does, of course) and that you foresee as an adventure in learning. After you have assessed your options, bring these before the Lord in prayer and ask him to direct your choice.

Surveying the Terrain

The next step is to survey the entire book for length and assess how quickly you can memorize it. Perhaps you can start at one verse per day, six days per week. I recommend taking one day off per week to keep from getting burned out or to take up the slack for days in which you are sick or exceptionally busy.

Here's an approach to surveying the terrain:

1. Count the total number of verses in the entire book (see appendix 1 for a table that lists the number of chapters and verses in each biblical book).
2. Divide that total number by the number of verses you will memorize per week. The answer is how many weeks the book should take you.

3. Look at a calendar and determine a tentative finish date.

4. If needed, add 10 percent so that you don't feel under too much pressure until you get used to this practice. For example, if you choose to memorize Ephesians, 155 verses at the rate of 6 verses per week will take you 26 weeks (or about 6 months). Adding 10 percent—that is, about 3 weeks—will give you a total of 29 weeks.

5. Optional: Make a covenant before the Lord that, with his help, you will memorize this book by this date. For example: "Lord, having sought you in prayer, I believe that you have led me to memorize (<u>name of the book</u>). I now dedicate myself to begin this task with your help and for your glory. I commit myself to memorizing this by (<u>date</u>)." Sign and date the covenant. Put it in a place where you can refer to it regularly when the times get tough.

The purpose of surveying the terrain is to mark out a reasonable pace that will make achievement of your goal a probability. It will show you how much you need to memorize every day and when you should finish. The covenant provides a practical help to encourage you to persevere.

6

Daily Procedures

Remember the Key: Repetition over Time

Repetition is the engine that drives everything. Saying a verse one hundred times in one day is not as helpful as saying it every day for one hundred days. The absolute key to successful Scripture memorization is repetition over a long time period. This is how you retain old verses while learning new ones. And it is during this long process that the Spirit grants the new insights into the passage that you yearn for.

Give Priority to Reviewing Old Verses

Always give priority to retaining old verses even over learning new ones. What's the point in memorizing new verses if you don't hold onto the old ones? This doesn't mean that you need to re-memorize the old ones but that you should begin every day's work by reviewing them. Consider this to be what you must accomplish to earn the privilege of acquiring some precious new verses (work before play!).

Memorize the Verse Numbers (Optional)

I have found it well worth the extra effort to memorize the verse numbers as if they were part of each verse. This will prevent you from omitting verses or even whole paragraphs when you're reciting the entire book. It will also enable you to pick out individual verses to quote to someone for ministry or evangelistic purposes. Finally, it will help you to recall the verses as you are reading Christian books that cite them. You won't have to look them up.

For example, the verse numbers for Ephesians 1:1–3 would be said like this: "*One-one* Paul, an apostle of Christ Jesus by the will of God, to the saints who are in Ephesus, and are faithful in Christ Jesus: *one-two* Grace to you and peace from God our Father and the Lord Jesus Christ. *one-three* Blessed be the God and Father of our Lord Jesus Christ . . ." And so on. Longer verse numbers are no different. Ephesians 6:11 would be "*six-eleven* Put on the whole armor of God, that you may be able to stand against the schemes of the devil." Acts 27:25–26 would be "*twenty-seven twenty-five* So take heart, men, for I have faith in God that it will be exactly as I have been told. *twenty-seven twenty-six* But we must run aground on some island."

I realize that not everyone agrees that there is value in memorizing verse numbers, and I respect that. But I have found that it actually makes memorization easier in the long run.

Photograph the Verse with Your Eyes

Memorization is partly visual. This is not to say that blind people can't memorize the Bible but that the memorization process is connected closely to the eyes. Read each new verse ten times, looking at each word as though photographing it with your eyes. I can still remember where some particular verses were on the page of the Bible I first used to memorize them. Burn each verse into your brain with your eyes.

Say the Verse out Loud

Another help in memorizing is to say the verse out loud to yourself. The additional sensory input to your brain helps the memorization process. You don't have to speak loudly, just loud enough to hear it. Also, try putting some feeling and interpretation into reciting the verses. This is actually a form of meditation on the verses as you are learning them.

Sample Daily Procedure

The following is an example of how someone could go about memorizing Ephesians at the rate of one verse per day:

Day 1

- Read Ephesians 1:1 out loud ten times, looking at each word as if photographing it with your eyes. Include the verse number if you choose. Then cover the page and recite it ten times. You're done for the day.

Day 2

- *Yesterday's verse first.* Recite yesterday's verse, Ephesians 1:1, ten times, including the verse number if you choose. Look in the Bible if you need to, just to refresh your memory.
- *New verse.* Read Ephesians 1:2 out loud ten times, looking at each word as if photographing it with your eyes. Include the verse number if you choose. Then cover the page and recite it ten times. You're done for the day.

Day 3

- *Yesterday's verse first.* Recite yesterday's verse, Ephesians 1:2, ten times, including the verse number if you choose. Look in the Bible if you need to, just to refresh your memory.
- *Old verses, all together.* Recite Ephesians 1:1–2 together once, including the verse numbers if you choose.

- *New verse.* Read Ephesians 1:3 out loud ten times, looking at each word as if photographing it with your eyes. Include the verse number if you choose. Then cover the page and recite it ten times. You're done for the day.

Day 4

- *Yesterday's verse first.* Recite yesterday's verse, Ephesians 1:3, ten times, including the verse number if you choose. Look in the Bible if you need to, just to refresh your memory.
- *Old verses, all together:* Recite Ephesians 1:1–3 together once, including the verse numbers if you choose.
- *New verse.* Read Ephesians 1:4 out loud ten times, looking at each word as if photographing it with your eyes. Include the verse number if you choose. Then cover the page and recite it ten times. You're done for the day.

This cycle would continue through the entire book. Obviously, the "old verses, all together" stage will soon swell to take most of the time. That's exactly the way it should be. The entire book of Ephesians can be read at a reasonable rate in less than fifteen minutes. Therefore, the "old verses, all together" stage of your review should not take longer than that on any given day. Do it with the Bible ready at hand in case you draw a blank or get stuck; there's no shame in looking, and it actually helps to nail down troublesome verses.

Your sixtieth day (taking eight days off in that sixty-day span means you're on your fifty-second new verse, which would be Eph. 3:7) should look like this:

Day 60

- *Yesterday's verse first.* Recite yesterday's verse, Ephesians 3:6, ten times, including the verse number if you choose. Look in the Bible if you need to, just to refresh your memory.
- *Old verses, all together*: Recite Ephesians 1:1–3:6 together once, including the verse numbers if you choose. Look in the Bible if you need to, so this process won't take too long.
- *New verse.* Read Ephesians 3:7 out loud ten times, looking at each word as if photographing it with your eyes. Include the verse number if you choose. Then cover the page and recite it ten times. You're done for the day.

See appendix 2 for a memorization plan for the book of Ephesians.

7

Dealing with Challenges

THINGS DON'T ALWAYS GO SMOOTHLY. Life happens. Our machinelike progress sometimes breaks down. Our memories fail. We can get discouraged and go into dormant patches in which we memorize no verses for a while. What should we do about all of this? I want to offer encouragement for dealing with three challenges: (1) weeding the garden, (2) sanding the rough spots, and (3) recovering from a delay.

Weeding the Garden

As you recite a book over a long period of time without looking at the Bible, you will gradually begin to make little mistakes or leave verses out (again, this is why memorizing verse numbers is so helpful). In other words, weeds will start to grow in the garden of your mind. However, to weed the garden, read through the book once per week, looking at each verse carefully with your eyes. Do this in lieu of your "old verses, all together" daily task. This simple discipline will correct errors, weeding the garden.

Sanding the Rough Spots

Some portions of a book may be especially difficult. As you recite the verses, you may find that you need to look at the Bible more than usual to refresh your memory, even after many recitations, weeks into the process. When that happens to me, I hunker down and focus on that chapter or portion with special focus. Simply put, I give it more time and more hard labor. I may choose to recite that chapter or portion ten times—instead of the single daily recitation—for as many days as it takes. It's like making a piece of furniture and feeling the wood with your fingertips. The rough spots will need extra attention with the sandpaper. So it is with memorization: more repetitions, more work.

Also, as needed, I use mnemonic devices, sometimes stringing together the first letters of a series of words or noting rhythms and rhymes. Maybe you would need to write that portion down by hand and say it out loud while you write. Do whatever it takes. I consider something memorized when I can get up in the morning and, without looking at the Bible, say that chapter fluidly, without hesitation, with at least a 90 percent accuracy rate.

Recovering from a Delay

Sometimes you get away from a book for a stretch of time, maybe even for weeks. Maybe you've been on vacation or Christmas break. Maybe you've been sick. Or maybe you've just gotten lazy and stopped memorizing. Now you want to get back into it, but your memory is cold as ice. What now?

When this happens to me, I usually start right where I left off and learn whatever the next new verse would have been. Then I read all the old verses together out loud from the Bible, looking away as often as I can. Then, if I have the time, I review the most recent verses—the chapter I have most recently finished, ten times (in the pattern of "sanding the rough spots"). I keep doing this until I have it down pat—which may take a week or more. Then, I go backward to give the same special focus to the chapter before that. (Meanwhile, I am reading all the old verses once per day out loud.) I find that the earliest chapters usually come back pretty quickly. And since I have picked up where I left off and resumed learning new verses, I am encouraged that I am making progress through the book.

8

Kissing the Book Goodbye
. . . to Learn Other Books

ALL ALONG THE WAY, you have been reviewing the old verses all together day after day. I believe you should continue to review old verses every day *for one hundred days*. If you have done your work well, after about the second week of saying old verses, you probably won't need to refer to the Bible while you do this. Thus, you can follow this step while in the shower, while driving, while washing dishes, while walking down the road, or while exercising. It will add no extra time to your busy schedule. Moreover, in this stage you begin to see the scope of the entire book of Ephesians (or whatever book you have memorized). You will see large themes that unite chapters together. You will see the flow of the argument. You will discover new things that you never knew before.

CHAPTER 8

But then, after you have completed the one hundredth day, you should drop the verses off. Kiss them goodbye! Why do I advocate this? So that you can move on to other books. I encourage you to do this memorization work for the rest of your life. And the goal is not so much to retain the books you've memorized as to learn in depth as much of Scripture as you can.

I have learned to *keep an accurate record of the date* on which I learned a verse and then to calculate how many days I've reviewed that verse. When I have reached one hundred days of review, I stop saying each verse. I am sadly aware that they will soon decay from my memory, and after a while I will not be able to recite many of them. That is part of the corruption of our physical nature through our mortal bodies. However, the truths are still embedded deep in my mind, and actually many verses stick with me permanently, long after I have ceased to review them. I am still extremely familiar with the whole book: I understand not only its overall message but also many of its details because of the time I've spent on it. Furthermore, I know that I can resume reciting it and fire up my memory again if I want to. But I know that there is a limit to what I can retain in active memory. If I restrict myself to that limit, I will never be able to learn another book of the Bible. I'll be finished.

Therefore, I urge you to do the same. Keep your own records, and at one hundred days of recitation, kiss each verse goodbye. Now that doesn't mean you will forget them entirely. The meaning of these passages will stick with you and so will your general knowledge of the whole book and its teachings. You will remember what you learned as you look at the page, and you will never forget the book's flow of thought or even the specific insights you've gained. You will continue to be able to read the paragraphs aloud when needed with deep insight and sensitivity, and you will know what you're looking for when you flip to the book to confirm a cross-reference. The Holy Spirit will be able to bring back to mind whatever verses he wants to use to convict you of sin, strengthen your heart, or prepare you for witnessing. It's all still there—it's just subterranean now. If you should ever choose to return and upload it again, it will be far easier than if you'd never memorized it before.

The reason you kiss the book goodbye is to free you up to learn new books without requiring a major change in your lifestyle—entering a Scripture memorization monastery in which all you do with your life is memorize! For the sake of all the new insights you will gain by learning a new book of the Bible, you let go of the book and allow it to sink to the subterranean level. There will always be more memorization work you can do. The Bible is a vast universe to explore. *So keep learning new books.*

9

Memorizing Long Books
and Memorizing Faster

AFTER YOU'VE TAKEN SIX MONTHS with Ephesians at the rate of one verse per day, you may feel that you're ready to memorize a longer book. If, for example, you memorized Romans, you would be looking at 433 verses. At the rate of one verse per day, that's close to a year and a half (with a 10 percent fudge factor added in). That time period may be too long for you. You might be ready to pick up the pace instead. When I memorized the Gospel of Matthew, I did it at the rate of 36 verses per week—six per day, six days per week. It took me about nine months since I didn't maintain that pace the whole time. But Matthew is 1068 verses long. A verse per day would have been much too slow. Let's look at how to do multiple verses in a single day:

Day 1

- Read Matthew 1:1 out loud ten times, looking at each word as if photographing it with your eyes. Include the verse number if you choose. Then cover the page and recite it ten times. Repeat for 1:2–6, including the verse numbers if you choose. Then recite Matthew 1:1–6 ten times. You're done for the day.

Day 2

- *Yesterday's verses first.* Recite yesterday's verses, Matthew 1:1–6, ten times, including the verse numbers if you choose. Look in the Bible if you need to, just to refresh your memory.
- *New verses.* Read Matthew 1:7 out loud ten times, looking at each word as if photographing it with your eyes. Again, include the verse numbers if you choose. Then cover the page and recite it ten times. Repeat for 1:8–12. Then recite Matthew 1:7–12 ten times. You're done for the day.

Day 3

- *Yesterday's verses first.* Recite yesterday's verses, Matthew 1:7–12, ten times, including the verse numbers if you choose. Look in the Bible if you need to, just to refresh your memory.

- *Old verses, all together*: Recite Matthew 1:1–12 once.
- *New verses.* Read Matthew 1:13 out loud ten times, looking at each word as if photographing it with your eyes. Again, include the verse numbers if you choose. Then cover the page and recite it ten times. Repeat for 1:14–18. Then recite Matthew 1:13–18 ten times. You're done for the day.

Day 4

- *Yesterday's verses first.* Recite yesterday's verses, Matthew 1:13–18, ten times, including the verse numbers if you choose. Look in the Bible if you need to, just to refresh your memory.
- *Old verses, all together*: Recite Matthew 1:1–18 once.
- *New verses.* Read Matthew 1:19 out loud ten times, looking at each word as if photographing it with your eyes. Again, include the verse numbers if you choose. Then cover the page and recite it ten times. Repeat for 1:20–24. Then recite Matthew 1:19–24 ten times. You're done for the day.

The ongoing review (the "old verses, all together" stage) would get immense if you didn't "kiss verses goodbye"! After you've said each verse for one hundred days, drop them off the backside as you make progress forward. In this way, you can move through a long book like the Gospel of Matthew or Ezekiel without becoming overwhelmed.

Conclusion

MY PRAYER IS THAT GOD will raise up a generation of people who do this labor, thus presenting themselves to God as those approved, workers who do not need to be ashamed and who rightly handle the word of truth (2 Tim. 2:15). Your soul will be eternally enriched. You will store up treasure in heaven and be an orchard of fruit for your brothers and sisters in Christ. Both unbelievers and struggling churches are in deep need of the meat of God's word and of those qualified to give it to them. May God bless your diligence and perseverance.

Appendix 1

Number of Chapters and Verses in Each Biblical Book[1]

Book	Chapters	Verses	Book	Chapters	Verses
OLD TESTAMENT			1 Kings	22	816
Genesis	50	1,533	2 Kings	25	719
Exodus	40	1,213	1 Chronicles	29	942
Leviticus	27	859	2 Chronicles	36	822
Numbers	36	1,288	Ezra	10	280
Deuteronomy	34	959	Nehemiah	13	406
Joshua	24	658	Esther	10	167
Judges	21	618	Job	42	1,070
Ruth	4	85	Psalms	150	2,461
1 Samuel	31	810	Proverbs	31	915
2 Samuel	24	695	Ecclesiastes	12	222

1 Based on the text and versification of the ESV. Verse counts in other translations may differ slightly.

Book	Chapters	Verses	Book	Chapters	Verses
Song of Solomon	8	117	Acts	28	1,003
Isaiah	66	1,292	Romans	16	432
Jeremiah	52	1,364	1 Corinthians	16	437
Lamentations	5	154	2 Corinthians	13	257
Ezekiel	48	1,273	Galatians	6	149
Daniel	12	357	Ephesians	6	155
Hosea	14	197	Philippians	4	104
Joel	3	73	Colossians	4	95
Amos	9	146	1 Thessalonians	5	89
Obadiah	1	21	2 Thessalonians	3	47
Jonah	4	48	1 Timothy	6	113
Micah	7	105	2 Timothy	4	83
Nahum	3	47	Titus	3	46
Habakkuk	3	56	Philemon	1	25
Zephaniah	3	53	Hebrews	13	303
Haggai	2	38	James	5	108
Zechariah	14	211	1 Peter	5	105
Malachi	4	55	2 Peter	3	61
Total in Old			1 John	5	105
Testament	*929*	*23,145*	2 John	1	13
			3 John	1	15
NEW TESTAMENT			Jude	1	25
Matthew	28	1,067	Revelation	22	404
Mark	16	673	*Total in New*		
Luke	24	1,149	*Testament*	*260*	*7,941*
John	21	878	*Total in Bible*	*1,189*	*31,086*

Appendix 2

Ephesians Memorization Plan

Day #	Date	Today's verse (10 times)	Previous verse (10 times)	Cummulative review (1 time)
1	Jan. 1	1:1	N/A	N/A
2	Jan. 2	1:2	1:1	1:1–2
3	Jan. 3	1:3	1:2	1:1–3
4	Jan. 4	1:4	1:3	1:1–4
5	Jan. 5	1:5	1:4	1:1–5
6	Jan. 6	1:6	1:5	1:1–6
7	Jan. 7	Day off		
8	Jan. 8	1:7	1:6	1:1–7
9	Jan. 9	1:8	1:7	1:1–8
10	Jan. 10	1:9	1:8	1:1–9
11	Jan. 11	1:10	1:9	1:1–10
12	Jan. 12	1:11	1:10	1:1–11
13	Jan. 13	1:12	1:11	1:1–12

Day #	Date	Today's verse (10 times)	Previous verse (10 times)	Cummulative review (1 time)
14	Jan. 14	Day off		
15	Jan. 15	1:13	1:12	1:1–13
16	Jan. 16	1:14	1:13	1:1–14
17	Jan. 17	1:15	1:14	1:1–15
18	Jan. 18	1:16	1:15	1:1–16
19	Jan. 19	1:17	1:16	1:1–17
20	Jan. 20	1:18	1:17	1:1–18
21	Jan. 21	Day off		
22	Jan. 22	1:19	1:18	1:1–19
23	Jan. 23	1:20	1:19	1:1–20
24	Jan. 24	1:21	1:20	1:1–21
25	Jan. 25	1:22	1:21	1:1–22
26	Jan. 26	1:23	1:22	1:1–23
27	Jan. 27	2:1	1:23	1:1–2:1
28	Jan. 28	Day off		
29	Jan. 29	2:2	2:1	1:1–2:2
30	Jan. 30	2:3	2:2	1:1–2:3
31	Jan. 31	2:4	2:3	1:1–2:4
32	Feb. 1	2:5	2:4	1:1–2:5
33	Feb. 2	2:6	2:5	1:1–2:6
34	Feb. 3	2:7	2:6	1:1–2:7
35	Feb. 4	Day off		
36	Feb. 5	2:8	2:7	1:1–2:8
37	Feb. 6	2:9	2:8	1:1–2:9
38	Feb. 7	2:10	2:9	1:1–2:10
39	Feb. 8	2:11	2:10	1:1–2:11
40	Feb. 9	2:12	2:11	1:1–2:12
41	Feb. 10	2:13	2:12	1:1–2:13

Day #	Date	Today's verse (10 times)	Previous verse (10 times)	Cummulative review (1 time)
42	Feb. 11	Day off		
43	Feb. 12	2:14	2:13	1:1–2:14
44	Feb. 13	2:15	2:14	1:1–2:15
45	Feb. 14	2:16	2:15	1:1–2:16
46	Feb. 15	2:17	2:16	1:1–2:17
47	Feb. 16	2:18	2:17	1:1–2:18
48	Feb. 17	2:19	2:18	1:1–2:19
49	Feb. 18	Day off		
50	Feb. 19	2:20	2:19	1:1–2:20
51	Feb. 20	2:21	2:20	1:1–2:21
52	Feb. 21	2:22	2:21	1:1–2:22
53	Feb. 22	3:1	2:22	1:1–3:1
54	Feb. 23	3:2	3:1	1:1–3:2
55	Feb. 24	3:3	3:2	1:1–3:3
56	Feb. 25	Day off		
57	Feb. 26	3:4	3:3	1:1–3:4
58	Feb. 27	3:5	3:4	1:1–3:5
59	Feb. 28	3:6	3:5	1:1–3:6
60	Mar. 1	3:7	3:6	1:1–3:7
61	Mar. 2	3:8	3:7	1:1–3:8
62	Mar. 3	3:9	3:8	1:1–3:9
63	Mar. 4	Day off		
64	Mar. 5	3:10	3:9	1:1–3:10
65	Mar. 6	3:11	3:10	1:1–3:11
66	Mar. 7	3:12	3:11	1:1–3:12
67	Mar. 8	3:13	3:12	1:1–3:13
68	Mar. 9	3:14	3:13	1:1–3:14
69	Mar. 10	3:15	3:14	1:1–3:15

Day #	Date	Today's verse (10 times)	Previous verse (10 times)	Cummulative review (1 time)
70	Mar. 11	Day off		
71	Mar. 12	3:16	3:15	1:1–3:16
72	Mar. 13	3:17	3:16	1:1–3:17
73	Mar. 14	3:18	3:17	1:1–3:18
74	Mar. 15	3:19	3:18	1:1–3:19
75	Mar. 16	3:20	3:19	1:1–3:20
76	Mar. 17	3:21	3:20	1:1–3:21
77	Mar. 18	Day off		
78	Mar. 19	4:1	3:21	1:1–4:1
79	Mar. 20	4:2	4:1	1:1–4:2
80	Mar. 21	4:3	4:2	1:1–4:3
81	Mar. 22	4:4	4:3	1:1–4:4
82	Mar. 23	4:5	4:4	1:1–4:5
83	Mar. 24	4:6	4:5	1:1–4:6
84	Mar. 25	Day off		
85	Mar. 26	4:7	4:6	1:1–4:7
86	Mar. 27	4:8	4:7	1:1–4:8
87	Mar. 28	4:9	4:8	1:1–4:9
88	Mar. 29	4:10	4:9	1:1–4:10
89	Mar. 30	4:11	4:10	1:1–4:11
90	Mar. 31	4:12	4:11	1:1–4:12
91	Apr. 1	Day off		
92	Apr. 2	4:13	4:12	1:1–4:13
93	Apr. 3	4:14	4:13	1:1–4:14
94	Apr. 4	4:15	4:14	1:1–4:15
95	Apr. 5	4:16	4:15	1:1–4:16
96	Apr. 6	4:17	4:16	1:1–4:17
97	Apr. 7	4:18	4:17	1:1–4:18

Day #	Date	Today's verse (10 times)	Previous verse (10 times)	Cummulative review (1 time)
98	Apr. 8	Day off		
99	Apr. 9	4:19	4:18	1:1–4:19
100	Apr. 10	4:20	4:19	1:1–4:20
101	Apr. 11	4:21	4:20	1:1–4:21
102	Apr. 12	4:22	4:21	1:1–4:22
103	Apr. 13	4:23	4:22	1:1–4:23
104	Apr. 14	4:24	4:23	1:1–4:24
105	Apr. 15	Day off		
106	Apr. 16	4:25	4:24	1:1–4:25
107	Apr. 17	4:26	4:25	1:1–4:26
108	Apr. 18	4:27	4:26	1:1–4:27
109	Apr. 19	4:28	4:27	1:1–4:28
110	Apr. 20	4:29	4:28	1:1–4:29
111	Apr. 21	4:30	4:29	1:1–4:30
112	Apr. 22	Day off		
113	Apr. 23	4:31	4:30	1:1–4:31
114	Apr. 24	4:32	4:31	1:1–4:32
115	Apr. 25	5:1	4:32	1:1–5:1
116	Apr. 26	5:2	5:1	1:1–5:2
117	Apr. 27	5:3	5:2	1:1–5:3
118	Apr. 28	5:4	5:3	1:1–5:4
119	Apr. 29	Day off		
120	Apr. 30	5:5	5:4	1:1–5:5
121	May 1	5:6	5:5	1:1–5:6
122	May 2	5:7	5:6	1:1–5:7
123	May 3	5:8	5:7	1:1–5:8
124	May 4	5:9	5:8	1:1–5:9
125	May 5	5:10	5:9	1:1–5:10

Day #	Date	Today's verse (10 times)	Previous verse (10 times)	Cummulative review (1 time)
126	May 6	Day off		
127	May 7	5:11	5:10	1:1–5:11
128	May 8	5:12	5:11	1:1–5:12
129	May 9	5:13	5:12	1:1–5:13
130	May 10	5:14	5:13	1:1–5:14
131	May 11	5:15	5:14	1:1–5:15
132	May 12	5:16	5:15	1:1–5:16
133	May 13	Day off		
134	May 14	5:17	5:16	1:1–5:17
135	May 15	5:18	5:17	1:1–5:18
136	May 16	5:19	5:18	1:1–5:19
137	May 17	5:20	5:19	1:1–5:20
138	May 18	5:21	5:20	1:1–5:21
139	May 19	5:22	5:21	1:1–5:22
140	May 20	Day off		
141	May 21	5:23	5:22	1:1–5:23
142	May 22	5:24	5:23	1:1–5:24
143	May 23	5:25	5:24	1:1–5:25
144	May 24	5:26	5:25	1:1–5:26
145	May 25	5:27	5:26	1:1–5:27
146	May 26	5:28	5:27	1:1–5:28
147	May 27	Day off		
148	May 28	5:29	5:28	1:1–5:29
149	May 29	5:30	5:29	1:1–5:30
150	May 30	5:31	5:30	1:1–5:31
151	May 31	5:32	5:31	1:1–5:32
152	Jun. 1	5:33	5:32	1:1–5:33
153	Jun. 2	6:1	5:33	1:1–5:34

Day #	Date	Today's verse (10 times)	Previous verse (10 times)	Cummulative review (1 time)
154	Jun. 3	Day off		
155	Jun. 4	6:2	6:1	1:1–6:2
156	Jun. 5	6:3	6:2	1:1–6:3
157	Jun. 6	6:4	6:3	1:1–6:4
158	Jun. 7	6:5	6:4	1:1–6:5
159	Jun. 8	6:6	6:5	1:1–6:6
160	Jun. 9	6:7	6:6	1:1–6:7
161	Jun. 10	Day off		
162	Jun. 11	6:8	6:7	1:1–6:8
163	Jun. 12	6:9	6:8	1:1–6:9
164	Jun. 13	6:10	6:9	1:1–6:10
165	Jun. 14	6:11	6:10	1:1–6:11
166	Jun. 15	6:12	6:11	1:1–6:12
167	Jun. 16	6:13	6:12	1:1–6:13
168	Jun. 17	Day off		
169	Jun. 18	6:14	6:13	1:1–6:14
170	Jun. 19	6:15	6:14	1:1–6:15
171	Jun. 20	6:16	6:15	1:1–6:16
172	Jun. 21	6:17	6:16	1:1–6:17
173	Jun. 22	6:18	6:17	1:1–6:18
174	Jun. 23	6:19	6:18	1:1–6:19
175	Jun. 24	Day off		
176	Jun. 25	6:20	6:19	1:1–6:20
177	Jun. 26	6:21	6:20	1:1–6:21
178	Jun. 27	6:22	6:21	1:1–6:22
179	Jun. 28	6:23	6:22	1:1–6:23
180	Jun. 29	6:24	6:23	1:1–6:24